I Dream of a Church

by Ian Grant Spong

Contents

Prelude

I dream of a church where Jesus is its active Head and what He taught is the core of its values. I dream of a church where the leadership is chosen by His will not the will of man. I dream of a church that takes the advice of ancient fathers, Protestant reformers and contemporary preachers, but compares it to the Bible rather than vain traditions or worldly cultural values. I dream of a church which thirsts for prayer and hearing the Bible expounded. I dream of a church that is not just a social club worshiping the cultures and politics of this world, but seeks the values of a kingdom not from here. I dream of a church which has faith in the word of God and not the values of a lost world. I dream of a church that knows why it exists and Who it obeys, to glorify Jesus.

Twigs

Every church on the planet has twigs of doctrine, ideas formulated since Jesus and the Apostles walked this earth. Whether these ideas were formulated by various church councils, ancient or modern cultures, Protestant Reformers, or popular fads, they must be placed a distant second to New

Testament teachings. The problem is that these twigs of doctrine too often become idols which should be discarded entirely, because they block out the Sun of Righteousness, Jesus (Malachi 4:2), or take the focus away from the teachings of Jesus (Matthew 28:20). I dream of a church that would smash the idols of vain traditions and focus so much on the teachings of Jesus and the Apostles, that 2,000 years of doctrinal twigs will fade into insignificance.

Tolerance vs Coercion

One area of frustration for the biblical Christian is the lack of tolerance towards those who actually believe the Bible. How many Christians keep their mouths shut about certain twigs of doctrine that discomfort their faith? How many feel they will be coerced to believe something that neither Jesus nor the Apostles taught if they dare reveal their deepest faith? I dream of a church where the trunk of the tree, the teachings of Jesus and the Apostles, is emphasized, not the twigs, and that tolerance for individual faith within those biblical guidelines is encouraged.

Trunk

Every orthodox (right teaching) church on the planet teaches the essential trunk of the tree doctrines of the faith. If we listen to a sermon by a Catholic, Eastern Orthodox, Oriental Orthodox, or Protestant which expounds the Gospels, they sound very similar. The differences will be when people toot their own denominational horn, or spew out their bigotry against one or the other because of disagreements over a plethora of twigs of doctrine. However, the trunk is amazingly the same in all churches, cults excepted. I dream of a church that focuses on the trunk of the tree and lets the twigs fall off and die without lifegiving sap.

Jesus

For 2000 years Jesus has built His Church. It has been far from perfect, not because Jesus failed, but because He is filled with grace towards His often very weak and sinful people. We are not saints, holy people because we are perfect, but because we have asked for and received God's forgiveness. Let's not be naïve in thinking that we will begin a new church and succeed where our forebears have failed. We too will introduce silly ideas and faulty theology. I dream of a church where this sifting largely succeeds.

What about those who sincerely desired to go back to the faith once delivered, but ended up introducing 19th century legalism and modern liberalism that neither Jesus nor the Apostles taught? How can we be so arrogant to believe that we will not fail in some similar manner. While the goal remains, so too will we fail at some things. I dream of a church that contends *"earnestly for the faith which was once for all delivered to the saints" (Jude 1:3 NKJV)* and eagerly repents of anything that does not fit that description.

On another note, we need to learn the difference between description and prescription. Descriptions of events are not always a prescription as to how we should do things. We must be careful not to discount God's inspiration or God-given freedom to choose between right alternatives. For instance, Jesus was circumcised, kept Sabbath, walked everywhere and was unmarried. That is a description but not a prescription, because none of that is a command for the church. I dream of a church that encourages freedom of conscience in areas not commanded by Jesus or the Apostles.

Let's learn to distinguish between clear commands, inspired activity, freedom of choice and church sins. We could also ask ourselves when something was Holy Spirit inspired, whether or not God means that we should always do things that way. So, let's ask God for discernment in this process, and please feel free to agreeably disagree with this presentation. It is not the infallible word of God, but a contribution to an ongoing discussion. I dream of a church that openly encourages grace in non-essentials.

Jesus said that He will build His church (Matthew 16:18). So, we are not alone. We build with Jesus. Do we build our part on rock or sand (Matthew 7:24-29)? Do we build on another man's foundation (Romans 15:20)? Like wise master builders (1 Corinthians 3:10) do we use gold, silver and precious stones or wood, hay and stubble (1 Corinthians 3:12)? I dream of a church that does not again build some kind of legalistic bondage like that of religious leaders which Jesus confronted, but exercises the liberty which we have in Christ Jesus (Galatians 2:4, 18-19).

I dream of building a church with Jesus. What would that look like? None of us can wait until we and our theology are perfect, or we will miss the boat. We are all mere human beings trying as best we can, and though we take their advice onboard, we don't build on fallible ancient fathers, equally faulty Reformation leaders, or questionable modern fads. We build on the original foundation found in the Bible alone, *"the apostles and prophets with Christ Jesus himself as the cornerstone." (Ephesians 2:20 CEB).* It may sound cliché but I dream of a church where the Bible is our guide.

What will we build upon that foundation? Will we always build perfectly or sometimes wrongly and have to fix mistakes? Repentance is supposed to be lifelong. If we are not willing to change some things in 20, 40 or 60 years as we grow in grace and knowledge, we will just turn into modern Pharisees and Sadducees protecting our own vain traditions. Will we build with precious fireproof materials or cheap flammable materials? (1 Corinthians 3:12-13) I dream of a church that honors God by building, as best as humans can, with such precious materials that they will not burn up in times of fiery trial.

Preparation for Preparation

In a greater sense, the whole Old Testament period was preparation for the church. But, lest we fill too large a volume, let's begin by exploring the disciple-training ministry of Jesus.

The Gospels detail about three and a half years of preparation for the new church with the training of its foundational leaders. However, preparation for that preparation was also carried out by John the Baptist.

When beginning a new church, often there will be someone who prepares the way, who does not continue with the new church, as John the Baptist prepared for Jesus, but died too soon. The message that John brought is also very familiar.

"Repent, for the kingdom of heaven is at hand." For this is he who was spoken of by the prophet Isaiah when he said, "The voice of one crying in the wilderness: 'Prepare the way of the Lord; make his paths straight.'" (Matthew 3:2-3 ESV)

Fasting

Fasting is always a good preparation for a new church. We are not Jesus and nobody should fast as long as He did barring a miracle, but most healthy people can easily fast without solid food a day or two.

"After Jesus had gone without eating for forty days and nights, he was very hungry." (Matthew 4:2 CEV)

Notice that it does not say Jesus was thirsty, so it is possible that He drank at least water. I dream of a church built with prayer and fasting.

Repentance

What kind of message begins to build a church? We don't need to be overly stressed or concerned about reinventing the wheel. The message that Jesus preached is the best.

"From that time Jesus began to preach, and to say, Repent: for the kingdom of heaven is at hand." (Matthew 4:17 KJV)

Repentance literally means to have a change of heart or mind, but it must also have fruits, meaning a turning FROM sin and TO God. It's a simple message, but powerful. I dream of a church that actually repents of a thousand do's and don'ts, of doctrinal idols, that overshadow and bury the teachings of Jesus.

Choosing Leaders

Jesus did not ask for volunteers nor did He take a congregational vote, when He chose His disciples. We may not have the same opportunity or marvellous response that Jesus had when He said, Come follow me. I doubt that many modern missionaries and church planters will simply rock up and find the same zeal, that people immediately drop tools and follow them. However, some do prioritize church over worldly pursuits, indicating that they may be ready to begin discipleship training. It may be a pipe dream, but I do dream of a church where its leaders are even just half as dedicated as those first disciples.

The entire sermon on the mount is in one way shape or form relevant to beginning a new church, yet here are a few points that stand out as directly applicable.

Who are We Serving

We often think of serving a local church and somewhere along the line money is needed for something, yet we must always remember that money is just a tool; it is God whom we serve.

"No one can serve two masters; for either he will hate the one and love the other, or he will be devoted to one and despise the other. You cannot serve God and wealth." (Matthew 6:24 NASB)

Build on the Rock

We also need to remember that we want to build any church on a rock, and that rock is *"everyone who hears these words of mine and puts them into practice"* (Matthew 7:24-29). So, in starting a new church, it is the practical words of Jesus that will be the best help. I dream of a church built on Jesus' words.

The Workers are Few

Most church work is done by a few dedicated people. *"The harvest truly is plentiful, but the laborers are few. Therefore pray the Lord of the harvest to send out laborers into His harvest." (Matthew 9:37b-38 NKJV)* I dream of a church where everyone gets involved.

Missionary Work

Missionary work is primarily starting new churches. The original missionaries were gifted with miracles rarely experienced today and often faked by counterfeits. Yet, there is something that we can all learn.

"If any household or town refuses to welcome you or listen to your message, shake its dust from your feet as you leave." (Matthew 10:14 NLT)

Rejection is normal. Let's forget it and move on. Experienced sales people say they love the word "no" because it saves wasting time, and frees us to move on to the next prospect. Like sales, receptiveness to the Gospel is a numbers game. If only one in ten is responsive, we want to spend our time with that person, and move on as fast as possible from those who reject our message. I dream of a church that is outwardly focused on. spreading the Good News.

Parables

Like the seed scattered on the footpath, rocky soil, among thorns and in good soil, so too will our efforts only sometimes bear much fruit (Matthew 13:3-9, 18-23). Like the wheat and weeds, so too will those who do gather with us be a mixed bunch (vs 24-30, 36-43). Like the parable of the mustard seed, a new church begins very small before becoming very large (vs 31-32). Like the parable of the leaven, take heart that our small efforts will multiply (vs 33-35). Like the parables of the hidden treasure and pearl of great price, we should remember that what we carry is the greatest treasure on earth (vs 44-46). Like the parable of the fishing net, the church will pick up all kinds of people, both good and bad (vs 47-51). I dream of a church that Jesus builds.

A Work of Faith

Like feeding the 5000 (Matthew 14:13-21), later 4000 (Matthew 15:29-39) and walking on water (Matthew 14:22-33), building a church is a work of faith. I dream of a church with strong faith.

Vain Traditions

As churches grow certain habits will become traditions. There are both good and bad traditions that churches can adopt. We ought to be careful that we do not break the command of God for the sake of our traditions (Matthew 15:3). Like the brass snake on a pole, a once helpful tradition can become an idol and must be destroyed (Numbers 21:6-9; 2 Kings 18:4). I dream of a church that discards traditions that have become idols.

I Will Build My Church

A most important statement about who will build the Christian Church is often overlooked because of another controversy surrounding the verse.

*"And I say also unto thee, That thou art Peter, and upon this rock **I will build my church**; and the gates of hell shall not prevail against it." (Matthew 16:18 KJV)*

Yes, Jesus said that He will build the Church. Though people also build, we must never forget who primarily builds and whose Church it is.

As an aside, most early church fathers who commented on this passage said that the "rock" was Peter's faith, a small number said it was Christ Himself or the apostles as a group. Only a very small number thought that "rock" referred to Peter. So, the greater number of early church fathers are not in agreement with the Roman interpretation of this particular passage of scripture.[1] I dream of a church that is willing to admit it was wrong.

Listen to Him

Though we learn from Moses and Elijah, God told the three disciples assembled on the mount of transfiguration, specifically to listen to Jesus, *"This is My beloved Son, in whom I am well pleased. Hear Him!" (Matthew 17:5)*. I dream of a church that studies the whole Bible, but makes what Jesus taught an important focus.

---

[1] Sakr, Johnny. *Peter, the Rock & Matthew 16:18: A Grammatical Analysis inc. Response to Tim Staples.* 2017. Academia.edu

If Your Brother Sins

The only other time that Jesus is recorded as mentioning the word church is regarding church discipline.

"Now if your brother sins, go and show him his fault in private; if he listens to you, you have gained your brother. But if he does not listen to you, take one or two more with you, so that on the testimony of two or three witnesses every matter may be confirmed. And if he refuses to listen to them, tell it to the church; and if he refuses to listen even to the church, he is to be to you as a Gentile and a tax collector." (Matthew 18:15-17 NASB)

This threefold approach to church discipline is well known among Christians, even if it is rarely practiced in full. It is a false assumption that this involves shunning. Would Jesus mean to treat the rebellious brother like the Pharisees treated people? Of course not. The unteachable parishioner should understand that he is outside God's will, and cannot be considered for any church leadership role, but is still to be treated with courtesy and Christian kindness.

Two or Three

Does Jesus ignore a gathering of two or three?

"Again, truly I tell you that if two of you on earth agree about anything they ask for, it will be done for them by my Father in heaven. For where two or three gather in my name, there am I with them." (Matthew 18:19-20 NIV) I dream of a church where everyone recognizes God in our midst.

Truth

Did Jesus promise that later generations of Christians would discover as yet unknown aspects of the truth, or was He making this promise just to the apostles?

"However, when He, the Spirit of truth, has come, He will guide you [plural] into all truth; for He will not speak on His own authority, but whatever He hears He will speak; and He will tell you [plural] things to come." (John 16:13 NKJV)

This was addressed to the apostles and not to later generations of the church. Changes or additions to what Jesus and the apostles taught within the New Testament is not addressed. Whether or not later ecumenical councils obeyed or disobeyed this directive is something for another discussion. However, the importance of the Bible must not be diminished or overshadowed. I dream of a church that honors the teachings of Jesus and the Apostles above all others.

Naked Ambition

When the mother of the two sons of Zebedee sought positions for her sons, this caused a great stir among the disciples (Matthew 20). Naked ambition causes many problems in churches, and yet the best thing that any missionary can do for a new church is to leave immediately after local leaders are trained, rather than continue to hang on in power. I dream of a church where indigenous leaders preach the Gospel in a manner relevant to their own culture, rather than becoming clones of a foreign missionary's culture.

Palm Sunday

One of the biggest lessons to learn from Palm Sunday is that Jesus rode into town on a donkey, not in a gold chariot or on an expensive thoroughbred (Matthew 21:1-11). I dream of a church where great humility is found among all leaders.

House of Prayer

When Jesus cleared the Temple of merchandising, His main complaint was that it should be a house of prayer (Matthew 21:13). I dream of a church where prayer is a real focus.

Ordination

Most churches prefer someone officially trained in their theology and ordained by denominational authorities. Yet, here we see that neither Jesus nor John the Baptist were officially ordained by men. Does that mean that we too should be independent? Not necessarily. It depends on where God calls us to serve. However, if I had to do it over again I would not want to be beholden to an organization of men, because that's what ordination requires. You must swear to their theological twigs which you either swallow whole, keep silent for the sake of peace or defile your conscience by pretending you agree in every detail. So, we should not automatically discount an independent preacher, who may be like John or Jesus, ordained by heaven rather than men (Matthew 21:23-27). I dream of a church where there is agreement on the essentials and an atmosphere of agreeable disagreement over twigs of doctrine can thrive, yet without divisive dissenters constantly undermining the peace.

Tenants

The parable of the tenants shows that sometimes those who occupy God's vineyard are dishonest with the Lord's affairs and even murderers. We must not retaliate in kind, but wait upon the Lord to set things right (Matthew 21:33-41). Just as the kingdom of God was taken away from those religious leaders, so too will God do to others who act like them (vs 42-46). I dream of a church with faithful stewards tending the vineyard of God.

The Wedding Banquet

The parable of the wedding banquet shows those starting new churches, that many will refuse to come, and that those who accept the invitation may be a motley mixed crew of both good and bad backgrounds (Matthew 22:1-14). I dream of a welcoming church where wealth and clothing are irrelevant.

Civil Governments

Though some churches choose not to cooperate with civil governments, Jesus showed that paying the imperial tax to Caesar was a good thing (Matthew 22:15-22). Though there are places where just being a Christian or owning a Bible is illegal, in most cases it is wise for new churches to have a reputation of cooperating with civil authorities. I dream of a church that cooperates with civil authorities, but is clear about not compromising Christian principles.

The Great Commandments

The focus of teaching in any new church must not be on vain traditions or wacky fads, but on the proven Great Commandments (Matthew 22:34-40). I dream of a church where love of God and neighbor is defined God's way, not the world's.

Seven Woes

All potential church leaders must beware that they enter dangerous positions whereby others have bound heavy loads on people's shoulders (Matthew 23:4), promoting their own egos with fancy clothing and demanding to be called by religious titles (vs 5-12). All potential leaders ought to study and be wary of seven woes that can accompany misuse of spiritual office (vs 13-32). I dream of church leaders who humbly recognize the Scribe and Pharisee within themselves.

Not Your Best Life Now

A popular but false Gospel is contradicted by Jesus, who warned that things will not always be pleasant for true Christians.

"You will be arrested, punished, and even killed. Because of me, you will be hated by people of all nations. Many will give up and will betray and hate each other. Many false prophets will come and fool a lot of people. Evil will spread and cause many people to stop loving others. But if you keep on being faithful right to the end, you will be saved." (Matthew 24:9-13 CEV)

This is not exactly the kind of message that will build a big, popular church, but it will build a church that is based upon truth rather than hollow lies, and it will build lives that can endure to the end. I dream of a church that is committed to Jesus, no matter what.

Virgins

Don't be surprised if the church that God builds through you contains both foolish and wise members, those who take extra oil of the Holy Spirit in their vessels, and those who don't, who will be told on that day *"Truly, I say to you, I do not know you." (Matthew 25:12 ESV)*

Warn them, and preach to them to *"Watch therefore, for ye know neither the day nor the hour wherein the Son of man cometh."* (vs 13) I dream of a church that shakes in its boots when it hears the parable of the wise and foolish virgins.

Talents

Warn them also that God gives various amounts of spiritual deposits from heaven, similar to five, two or one quantities of gold. Warn them that God expects a profit from these spiritual deposits and those who do nothing will be punished. *"For to everyone who has, more shall be given, and he will have an abundance; but from the one who does not have, even what he does have shall be taken away."* (Matthew 25:29 NASB) I dream of a church where everyone is using their talents.

Sheep and Goats

Warn the church also not to just be concerned with salvation and blessings for themselves, but to feed the hungry and thirsty, welcome the foreigner, clothe the naked, visit the sick, and go to the prisoner. *"The King will reply, 'Truly I tell you, whatever you did for one of the least of these brothers and sisters of mine, you did for me.'"* (Matthew 25:40 NIV) What of those who do not help the needy? *"And these will go away into everlasting punishment, but the righteous into eternal life." (vs 46 NKJV)* I dream of a church that treasures Jesus' values and is not swayed by politics.

Costly Giving

Teach the church that not every gift must be for the poor and needy, but also giving extravagantly to Jesus is appropriate. Let's not be like the disciples who said, *"It could have been sold for a high price and the money given to the poor." (Matthew 26:9 NLT)* Giving to the poor is balanced with a woman's generous gift to honor and bless Jesus. He said, *"I tell you the truth that wherever in the whole world this good news is announced, what she's done will also be told in memory of her." (Matthew 26:13 CEB)* I dream of a church that is extravagant in giving.

Betrayal

If Judas betrayed Jesus, let's not be naïve. We too will be betrayed at some point in our church life. Like Judas *"started looking for a good chance to betray Jesus" (Matthew 26:16 CEV)* so too can there be similar people in any church. I dream of a church that is not shocked when betrayal happens.

The Lord's Supper

As Jesus was about to become our Passover Lamb He gave new rituals to the church, using bread and wine, saying this is His body and blood (Matthew 26:26-28).

Though the bread Jesus used was unleavened Passover bread, any later instructions about it, never mandate leavened or unleavened. There is no adjective. It is just called bread.

A 19th century overreaction against the abuse of alcohol, plus the inventions of pasteurization and refrigeration, popularized grape juice among many churches. However, six months after the grape harvest, it is obvious that any grape juice was long fermented into wine. Jesus used wine.

I dream of a church that continues this rite in the simplicity that Jesus instituted it.

Denial

Let's not be too naïve about our developing church leaders. If Judas betrayed Jesus, most of the disciples fled and Peter denied Him three times (Matthew 26:30-35), don't expect perfection from church leaders. If Jesus' disciples all failed, so will leaders in any church at one time or another. It's just part of the human condition. I dream of a church that creates an atmosphere of grace towards the faults of its leaders and parishioners.

Brought before Councils

In some countries, those who start Christian churches may be betrayed and arrested like Jesus was (Matthew 26:47-56) and all their disciples may leave and flee (vs 56). They may be brought before religious councils like Jesus was (vs 57-68). The religious leaders may take counsel against them and seek to put them to death (Matthew 27:1-2). They may be brought before civil authorities to answer questions like Pilate did Jesus (vs 11-31). More Christians are killed for their faith today like Jesus was, than any other time in history. I dream of a church that prays for our brothers and sisters under state or religious persecution around the world.

The Great Commission

Part of the reason for starting new churches is because it is a natural result of obeying the great commission.

"Jesus came and told his disciples, 'I have been given all authority in heaven and on earth. Therefore, go and make disciples of all the nations, baptizing them in the name of the

Father and the Son and the Holy Spirit. **Teach these new disciples to obey all the commands I have given you.**'" *(Matthew 28:18-20a NLT)*

So the teaching curriculum that Jesus outlined had a particular focus *"and teach them to do everything I have told you." (CEV)* Where would we find that information? It is found primarily in the Gospels, that is why preparation for starting new churches includes knowing what we must teach.

Though the Holy Spirit came on Pentecost, Jesus also continues to be with His Church.

"And behold, I am with you always, to the end of the age." (Matthew 28:20 ESV)

Jesus has always been there as Head of the church. Just as before the church era, sin has continued to prevail in the church, but grace has prevailed even more. Even in the darkest times, Jesus did not fail His church, but has always made sure that the essentials for salvation were there. I dream of a church that never loses its focus on what's really important.

Jesus' Prayer for the Church

We could continue this discussion in Mark, Luke and John but that is an assignment for the reader to ask questions about the church in the rest of the Gospels. Ask: How is this relevant to the church God can build through us? One final thought before we get onto the practical experience of the early church, is found in John 17. Jesus prays for the church that is about to begin on Pentecost. Some highlights could be the following.

"that they may be one… the world hath hated them, because they are not of the world, even as I am not of the world. I pray not that thou shouldest take them out of the world, but that thou shouldest keep them from the evil… Sanctify them through thy truth: thy word is truth… that they may be one… " (KJV)

Sanctify is from the Greek word which means to make holy or make saints. Sainthood or holiness comes in part through God's truth. Unity and saintliness are important attributes of the Christian church. While we may become a separate and independent local church, we must never forget that God's grace is sufficient for a wide variety of churches and we must never allow a self-righteous spirit to dominate us.

"Beloved, while I was very diligent to write to you concerning our common salvation, I found it necessary to write to you exhorting you to contend earnestly for the faith which was once for all delivered to the saints." (Jude 1:3 NKJV)

I dream of a church that is so immersed in fighting for and defending this faith, that it does not have time to become self-righteous by comparing itself to others.

Pentecost

Let's continue our journey in Acts 2, with the first megachurch, a congregation of more than 3,000 people. What happened there that is relevant to how we would want to approach our new church?

Multicultural

The first thing we might notice, that may be relevant to planting a church, is that this is what today's generation might call a multicultural church, with people from all over.

"Parthians and Medes and Elamites, those dwelling in Mesopotamia, Judea and Cappadocia, Pontus and Asia, Phrygia and Pamphylia, Egypt and the parts of Libya adjoining Cyrene, visitors from Rome, both

Jews and proselytes, Cretans and Arabs ..." (Acts 2:9-11 NKJV)

I dream of a multicultural church where people of different races, languages and cultures are comfortable together because their new allegiance is to the kingdom of heaven more than any customs of this world.

Key Speaker

There is a clue that perhaps all the apostles said at least something.

"They were surprised and amazed, saying, 'Look, aren't all the people who are speaking Galileans, every one of them?'" (Acts 2:7 CEB)

However, one stands out as perhaps the keynote speaker, Peter.

"Peter stood with the eleven apostles and spoke in a loud and clear voice to the crowd: Friends and everyone else living in Jerusalem, listen carefully to what I have to say!" (Acts 2:14 CEV)

This may happen in a local church run by a board of elders, where one is particularly gifted in public speaking and others are not. It requires humility to stand aside and let the more gifted one lead, or even slowly hand over the reins as a younger one matures into a new role within the ministry of the church. We will notice that later with Barnabas and Paul. Will there be rivalry as occurred while the Apostles were in training?

"An argument arose among them as to which of them was the greatest." (Luke 9:46 ESV)

I dream of a church where this kind of tug-of-war does not exist, but that each promotes the other for the sake of the Gospel.

Church Unity

"And they continued stedfastly in the apostles' doctrine and fellowship, and in breaking of bread, and in prayers. And fear came upon every soul: and many wonders and signs were done by the apostles. And all that believed were together, and had all things common; And sold their possessions and goods, and parted them to all men, as every man had need. And they, continuing daily with one accord in the temple, and breaking bread from house to house, did eat their meat with gladness and singleness of heart, Praising God, and having favour with all the people. And the Lord added to the church daily such as should be saved." (Acts 2:42-47 KJV)

O that such singleness of heart would exist in every local church, but that might be a little unrealistic. Most churches seem to have some kind of personality conflicts over a thousand silly and unimportant things.

O that genuine wonders and signs would be done in every new church, but alas that too does not happen all the time, and when it does, it is often reported to have been faked.

O that we might be strong enough in faith to share our possessions as they did. I think that most of us, at least in the west, will probably ignore that passage and quickly move on as if nothing was written or make quick excuses. So, let's leave that there for our consciences to deal with.

I dream of a church where people uplift those with greater gifts, where genuine miracles occur, not fakes, and where people are known for outrageous generosity.

Build on Christ

Church growth by itself means nothing. The Ba'al worshippers that Isaiah faced were far more numerous than he (Isaiah 18). Are we building human empires or God's kingdom? Some of the largest churches on earth are spiritually weak and starving. Some of the smallest hovels in distant lands are filled and satisfied with rich spiritual nourishment.

There are many large churches built upon a man, but they are weak for having been built on the wrong foundation. As soon as that man dies, the church falls apart if it was not built by Jesus. Only a church built on the Apostles, Prophets and Jesus being the cornerstone will last beyond the grave (Matthew 16:18). Let's follow the example of the Apostle Peter. He saw that people were astonished after a lame man was healed, but he was quick to give credit to God.

"But when Peter saw this, he replied to the people, 'Men of Israel, why are you amazed at this, or why are you staring at us, as though by our own power or godliness we had made him walk? The God of Abraham, Isaac, and Jacob, the God of our fathers, has glorified His servant Jesus, the one whom you handed over and disowned in the presence of Pilate, when he had decided to release Him.'" (Acts 3:12-13 NASB)

I dream of a church that honors and supports its human leaders, but worships Jesus.

Call to Repentance

Many today preach a message of just believing, but that builds a church without repentance. Peter, in his second sermon, called for repentance.

*"Now repent of your sins **and turn to God**, so that your sins may be wiped away." (Acts 3:19 NLT)*

Repent means to change our minds or hearts about sin, but it doesn't stop there. We also turn our lives away FROM sin and turn them TO God. When we preach this kind of message, then the church being built through us by Jesus Christ, will be headed in the right direction. Without repentance, we are no different from the demons who believe but don't repent or people who refused to listen to Jesus.

"Anyone who does not listen to him will be completely cut off from their people." (Acts 3:23 NIV)

A large part of Jesus' purpose was to teach repentance.

*"God sent his chosen Son to you first, because God wanted to bless you and make each one of you turn away **from your sins**." (Acts 3:26 CEV)*

I dream of a church that has the habit to turn away from sin and to God.

Authoritarian Religion

In many countries, if you are not part of the established religion, you will be harrassed. This is even the case in some countries with a national Christian church. Just because someone is a Christian, does not mean they are perfect, and Christian churches have been guilty even of atrocities in history, as Catholics and Protestants have even murdered each other. So, we should not be shocked when even fellow believers harass us.

"While Peter and John were speaking to the people, the priests, the captain of the temple guard, and the Sadducees confronted them. They were incensed that the apostles were teaching the people and announcing that the resurrection of the dead was happening because of Jesus." (Acts 4:1-2 CEB)

Another lesson about church growth in this chapter is that when harassment comes, sometimes growth does too. The early church grew from 3000 to 5000 during this time.

"But a lot of people who had heard the message believed it. So by now there were about five thousand followers of the Lord." (Acts 4:4 CEV)

I dream of a church that accepts the faith of Christians from other churches and treats them as brothers and sisters.

Work

One thing that many don't want to do is work. I admit, the following description seems like too much work for me.

"Every day they spent time in the temple and in one home after another. They never stopped teaching and telling the good news that Jesus is the Messiah." (Acts 5:42 CEV)

I dream of a church with enough enthusiastic and loyal preachers and teachers to fill all the needs throughout the week, leaving enough time to fast, pray and rest for all in leadership.

Proto-Deacons

One mistake that many church leaders make is mixing spiritual duties with physical. In modern countries there is a lot of red-tape involved in ministry. Health regulations, child-safety laws, wedding regulations, and many denominations seem to impose more and more loads of internal red tape. The paperwork alone can kill the spiritual side of ministry and so it is important that faithful and skilled deacon managers are found to free the elders from these duties.

A case in point is found in an early church management problem. How were needy people to be served equitably with daily food needs?

"And the twelve summoned the full number of the disciples and said, 'It is not right that we should give up preaching the word of God to serve tables. Therefore, brothers, pick out from among you seven men of good repute, full of the Spirit and of wisdom, whom we will appoint to this duty.'" (Acts 6:2-3 ESV)

Notice several things about this decision. This was a congregational decision, not an apostolic decision (vs 3a). Those chosen needed to have good reputations, be filled with the Holy Spirit and be wise (vs 3b). The reason for this division of labor is clear (vs 4). They chose all men (vs 5). Once the congregation had chosen them, the apostles would appoint or ordain them to this duty with the laying on of hands (vs 6). Though this is a description of what they did and not a commanded prescription for all future similar decisions, it does have the potential to be a precedent, if we notice similar reasoning afterwards.

"But we will give ourselves continually to prayer, and to the ministry of the word." (Acts 6:4 KJV)

Those of us who may be more oriented towards physical tasks can think that *"prayer and teaching the word" (NLT)* are not real work. Some people even make a joke that pastors only work one day a week. However, no church will do very well when *"prayer and the service of proclaiming the word" (CEB)* are neglected. An effective sermon requires at least 20 hours of preparation. The so-called Saturday night special, the bad habit of leaving the sermon until the night before, is guaranteed to be a weak failure, not blessed by God, except in rare emergencies.

The best sermon preparation is to begin long before the next sermon. A whole week for prayer, research and meditation is better than any last minute scramble. Prayer and ministry of the word are foundational to the spiritual health of a local church and must be seen as the most important work of those assigned to spiritual oversight. Churches that burden their elders with a litany of physical duties will be spiritually malnourished and weak. I dream of a church that completely understands the division of labor, and is blessed with skilled, willing deacons who take care of the physical management, so that the elders are free to focus on prayer and the ministry of the Word of God.

Opposition

See a church in town that does not have opposition and perhaps it is more worldly than Christian. Church planters should expect opposition from other religious leaders. They may have what I call exclusive franchise mentality, in that they act like a religious mafia that wants to be the only business in town. In some countries it is far worse than others, but be prepared. This was Stephen's experience.

"Now when they heard this, they were infuriated, and they began gnashing their teeth at him." (Acts 7:54 NASB)

I dream of a church that God has so blessed with spiritual fruit, that all opposition is overcome.

Power Seekers

Do churches ever experience someone trying to buy influence like Simon the Sorcerer? Over the years I've noticed an arrogance among some, often wealthier church members who believe that their worldly wisdom is wiser than that of poorer church members. They often assume that they are entitled to church leadership and though they may not attempt it as blatantly as Simon did, nevertheless they can often assume that their great contributions to church coffers has granted them the office. What did Simon do?

"And when Simon saw that through the laying on of the apostles' hands the Holy Spirit was given, he offered them money, saying, 'Give me this power also, that anyone on whom I lay hands may receive the Holy Spirit.'" (Acts 8:18-19 NKJV)

From this story we get the word *simony* meaning buying or selling a church office. In Simon's case, he seemed more interested in *"this power"* than receiving the Holy Spirit himself. This seems applicable to power plays within the Church throughout history. We see similar ambitious people, those who have bought an office, or seem otherwise more interested in lording it over others than letting the Holy Spirit lead. If we want our churches to be successful the shepherds of the flock must guard against anyone seeking power for selfish reasons.

May our leaders have the courage of Peter, who plainly answered Simon.

"May your money perish with you, because you thought you could buy the gift of God with money! You have no part or share in this ministry, because your heart is not right before God. Repent of this wickedness and pray to the Lord in the hope that he may forgive you for having such a thought in your heart. For I see that you are full of bitterness and captive to sin." (Acts 8:20-23 NIV)

I dream of a church where carnal ambition has not bought anyone an office, but that all those who serve make a valuable contribution to church health.

Deacon Authority

How much authority does a deacon have? Here we see a deacon, Philip baptize an Ethiopian and afterwards preach the Gospel.

"Now when they came up out of the water, the Spirit of the Lord caught Philip away, so that the eunuch saw him no more; and he went on his way rejoicing. But Philip was found at Azotus. And passing through, he preached in all the cities till he came to Caesarea." (Acts 8:39-40 NKJV)

I dream of a church where leaders are not stifled by silly lines of competition.

A Damascus Road Experience

As Jesus builds His Church, Christ's workers will experience much opposition even from religious leaders of other churches. God does not ask His Church to fight, but rely upon Jesus taking care of His flock. One such example is Jesus' confrontation with Saul the persecutor.

"As he was approaching Damascus on this mission, a light from heaven suddenly shone down around him. He fell to the ground and heard a voice saying to him, 'Saul! Saul! Why are you persecuting me?'" (Acts 9:3-4 NLT)

A sad legacy of church history is Christian persecuting Christian. It has not stopped and still takes place in various countries today. Opposition from non-Christians also continues worldwide, but according to *Open Doors* World Watch List[2], it has been the worst of all in places like North Korea, Afghanistan, Somalia, Libya, Pakistan, Eritrea, Yemen, Iran, Nigeria, India, Iraq, Syria, Sudan, Saudi Arabia, and so on. What happened as a result of Jesus confronting Saul?

---

[2] opendoors.org

"Then the church throughout Judea, Galilee and Samaria enjoyed a time of peace and was strengthened. Living in the fear of the Lord and encouraged by the Holy Spirit, it increased in numbers." (Acts 9:31 NIV)

This is not guaranteed to always be so, as our greatest hope is not in this life. The Church experienced ten major periods of persecution before the Emperor Constantine gave Christianity official state recognition. I dream of a church where those who are in opposition will have a similar Damascus road experience so that they too can be used mightily by God.

Willing to Listen

To whom should Christians preach the Gospel when Jesus is building a church through them? We often think of a certain target demographic, but the crowd that Jesus chooses will often be quite different from those we would normally associate with. What is a main ingredient among those who God is calling to His Church?

"Now therefore we are all here present in the sight of God to hear all things that have been commanded you by God." (Acts 10:33b WEB)

A readiness to listen is a key ingredient for many things in the church. Who should be in leadership, those who are not ready to listen, but have their own agendas? No! Who will make good candidates for members of the local church, those who want to turn the church around with worldly agendas? No! I dream of a church where everyone is eager to listen to Jesus and the Apostles.

A Benefit of Persecution

We may think that persecution has no positive benefits, but there is one, people who would have otherwise stayed home, scattered and carried the Gospel with them.

"Now those who were scattered because of the persecution that arose over Stephen traveled as far as Phoenicia and Cyprus and Antioch, speaking the word to no one except Jews. (Acts 11:19 ESV)

Did the word remain only among Jews?

"Among them were some people from Cyprus and Cyrene. They entered Antioch and began to proclaim the good news about the Lord Jesus also to Gentiles. The Lord's power was with them, and a large number came to believe and turned to the Lord." (Acts 11:20-21 CEB)

Like these ancient Christians, we too may have a preferred demographic to reach, but let's be ready to accept all who are willing to listen into our fellowship, no matter their background. I dream of a church that is willing to leave the comforts of home to spread the most important message on the planet.

Expect Miracles

Too many modern people no longer expect miracles. Yet, God still provides for His own. An example of God's provision in the early church was Peter's angelic release from Herod's prison and what happened to Herod sometime later?

"At once an angel from the Lord struck him down because he took the honor that belonged to God. Later, Herod was eaten by worms and died." (Acts 12:23 CEV)

I dream of a church that trusts God to free us from the grip of those who wish to undermine our ministry, and dispatch them in His own ways.

Simple Organization

What were the leaders of the church at Antioch called?

"Now there were in the church at Antioch prophets and teachers, Barnabas, Simeon who

was called Niger, Lucius of Cyrene, Manaen a lifelong friend of Herod the tetrarch, and Saul." *(Acts 13:1 ESV)*

The two offices of prophet and teacher, or singular office of prophet-teacher in this context refers to spiritual leadership of proclaiming and teaching God's word. We may be beginning to notice a difference between how deacons were chosen and elders. Two of them were ordained for missionary service not by a congregational decision, nor by their own individual decision, but directly by the Holy Spirit and confirmed with laying on of hands by the local church.

"As they ministered to the Lord, and fasted, the Holy Ghost said, Separate me Barnabas and Saul for the work whereunto I have called them. And when they had fasted and prayed, and laid their hands on them, they sent them away." (Acts 13:2-3 KJV)

I dream of a church that is not at a loss as to how to share the Gospel. The rest of Acts 13 reveals one way, by summarizing the story of God from Israel to Jesus.

Fleeing

When preaching the Gospel, sometimes it is necessary to leave town.

"And when an attempt was made by both the Gentiles and the Jews with their rulers, to treat them abusively and to stone them, they became aware of it and fled to the cities of Lycaonia, Lystra and Derbe, and the surrounding region; and there they continued to preach the gospel." (Acts 14:5-7 NASB)

Paul and Barnabas encourage us with the following words.

"We must go through many hardships to enter the kingdom of God …" (Acts 14:22b NIV).

I dream of a church that is willing to endure hardship because the Gospel is so precious.

Disputes

All churches will from time to time experience some kind of dispute.

Whether it is a rule of Old Testament law, a more recent church rule, or a matter of custom, there will be different opinions. In such cases, we need to remember that there is something far more important than our opinions on lesser matters.

"We believe that we are all saved the same way, by the undeserved grace of the Lord Jesus." (Acts 15:11 NLT)

Sometimes disputes arise over personnel. Paul and Barnabas had such a dispute.

"Their argument became so intense that they went their separate ways." (Acts 15:39a CEB)

I dream of a church that is not shocked by occasional disputes because church life is not, and never has been perfect.

Paul Evangelizing

There are many opportunities to spread the Gospel. At the time, the synagogue was open to public discussion.

"So as usual, Paul went there to worship, and on three Sabbaths he spoke to the people. He used the Scriptures" (Acts 17:2 CEV).

In Athens Paul also reasoned in the marketplace (vs 17). I really doubt that such openness would exist today in most places of worship of any religion. Yet, there are other opportunities available. Some have put up a table in a public place offering prayer or stand in a public place with a Bible in hand shouting to passers by. Others use the internet, door knocking, advertising, tracts and personal contact. Be prepared to be humiliated, as Paul experienced!

"some mocked. But others said, 'We will hear you again about this.'" (vs 32b ESV)

I dream of a church where members are unafraid to evangelize by any and every opportunity.

Missionaries

Elders called to pastoral care of a local congregation may stay a long time, but that was not the calling of a missionary apostle like Paul. In Corinth for example, *"he continued there a year and six months, teaching the word of God among them." (Acts 18:11 KJV) "Now Paul, when he had remained many days longer, took leave of the brothers and sisters and sailed away to Syria" (vs 18 NASB).*

I dream of a church where some are called to the apostolic ministry of missionary or church pioneer, so that the church of God will multiply exceedingly.

Time to Leave

In some places there may come a time to move on. For instance, *"Paul entered the synagogue and spoke boldly there for three months, arguing persuasively about the kingdom of God. But some of them became obstinate; they refused to believe and publicly maligned the Way. So Paul left them. He took the disciples with him and had discussions daily in the lecture hall of Tyrannus."* (Acts 19:8-9 NIV)

I dream of a church where, if people refuse to believe the word of God, those who do simply move out and meet elsewhere, valuing the Word of God above any habitual meeting place.

Unusual Miracles

I dream of a church where God works miracles even using small, anointed prayer cloths, as is the custom in some churches, following Paul's example.

"Now God worked unusual miracles by the hands of Paul, so that even handkerchiefs or aprons were brought from his body to the sick, and the diseases left them and the evil spirits went out of them." (Acts 19:11-12 NKJV)

Paul's Testimony

Paul taught both publicly and from house to house, *"testifying both to Jews and to Greeks repentance toward God, and faith toward our Lord Jesus."* (Acts 20:21 WEB)

I dream of a church that does not water the Gospel down by preaching faith without repentance.

Giving

In one of the few places outside the Gospels where Jesus is quoted, Paul said, *"You should remember the words of the Lord Jesus: 'It is more blessed to give than to receive.'"* (Acts 20:35 NLT)

I dream of a generous church that truly believes this.

Prophecy

In Tyre, Paul stayed with believers for a week and *"Compelled by the Spirit, they kept telling Paul not to go to Jerusalem."* (Acts 21:4 CEB)

I dream of a church where members are open to speak at the urging of the Holy Spirit.

Conspiracies

Faithful church leaders will at times run across people who conspire against them with slander and lies. Paul was no exception.

"When it was day, the Jews made a plot and bound themselves by an oath neither to eat nor drink till they had killed Paul. There were

more than forty who made this conspiracy." *(Acts 23:12-13 ESV)*

Jews from Jerusalem *"laid many and grievous complaints against Paul, which they could not prove."* *(Acts 25:7b KJV)*

I dream of a church that remains faithful to God despite such unethical conduct from within. May God forgive them, they don't know what they are doing.

Saints

Saints are not just the heroes of the faith, but every single Christian.

"To all who are in Rome, beloved of God, called [to be] saints" *(Romans 1:7 NKJV)*

Notice that the words "to be" are in italics in most Bibles. They are called saints. I dream of a church where there is no more reluctance to call God's holy people saints, for that is what we are, the moment our sins are forgiven.

Suppression

Wherever we are in the world, there is some measure of suppression of the truth. It exists in science, politics, and even in the church. Why do men cover up this most precious commodity?

"They exchanged the truth about God for a lie, and worshiped and served created things rather than the Creator—who is forever praised. Amen." (Romans 1:25 NIV)

If you think that intelligent, highly educated people are always logical, think again. The forensic evidence for God is everywhere. Design doesn't happen without a designer. DNA code doesn't happen without a code maker. Under divine inspiration, Paul calls out atheists by revealing their true motives for denying the obvious, an emotional desire to sin, in dozens of ways, rather than honest and logical conclusions about the available evidence (Romans 1:18-32). I dream of a church that is not ashamed while being assailed on all fronts by a world that mocks, represses, bans and in some countries, imprisons and murders Christians.

A Humble Church

I dream of a humble church that does not seek to justify its own sins by claiming infallibility for its official decisions.

"No one is righteous—not even one." (Romans 3:10b NLT)

No Special Churches

The "one true church syndrome" is ubiquitous. Some make this claim because of the "right" mode or age of baptism, the "right" worship day, the "right" doctrines, descent from the apostles, or some other form of human vanity. However, Paul has a different opinion.

"God treats everyone alike. He accepts people only because they have faith in Jesus Christ." (Romans 3:22 CEV)

I dream of a church that humbly recognizes Christians across a spectrum of faulty doctrines, because no church has perfect theology or a spotless history.

"What is left for us to brag about? Not a thing! Is it because we obeyed some law? No! It is because of faith." (Romans 3:27 CEV)

I dream of a church that does not brag about some church rules, or succession, but only in Christ Jesus (1 Corinthians 1:31).

Access Through Jesus

I dream of a church that teaches access to Jesus, not some authoritarianism of men.

"Therefore, since we have been made righteous through his faithfulness, we have

*peace with God **through our Lord Jesus Christ**. We have access by faith into this grace in which **we stand through him**, and we boast in the hope of God's glory."* (Romans 5:1-2 CEB)

I dream of a church that humbly teaches that an organization of mere mortals does not give that access to God, but that we stand through Jesus Christ.

Resurrection

Some modern churches no longer believe in the resurrection of Jesus, or mean by it some watered down version of what Christians have always believed. Don't be fooled by deceptive preaching! Resurrection is a core doctrine of the Christian faith.

"For if while we were enemies we were reconciled to God through the death of His Son, much more, having been reconciled, we shall be saved by His life." (Romans 5:10 NASB)

What is the faith of those who deny the resurrection?

"... if Christ wasn't raised to life, our message is worthless, and so is your faith." (1 Corinthians 15:14 CEV)

Why did most of the Apostles willingly die for something they knew was a lie? They didn't! They were witnesses. I dream of a church that truly believes in the resurrection of the dead, not counterfeits masquerading as Christianity.

Sin

Many modern churches don't want to hear about sin.

"They tell the seers, 'Stop seeing visions!' They tell the prophets, 'Don't tell us what is right. Tell us nice things. Tell us lies.'" (Isaiah 30:10 NLT)

Paul preached against sin unapologetically.

"Let not sin therefore reign in your mortal body, to make you obey its passions." (Romans 6:12 ESV)

I dream of a church that eagerly hears the hard sayings of the Bible as much as the easy ones.

"For the wages of sin is death; but the gift of God is eternal life through Jesus Christ our Lord." (Romans 6:23 KJV)

Mercy

Granted some pastors have committed adultery and worse, but most are sincerely trying to follow God. Paul, a minister of high rank, freely admitted his fallibility.

"For I know that good does not dwell in me, that is, in my flesh; for the willing is present in me, but the doing of the good is not. For the good that I want, I do not do, but I practice the very evil that I do not want." (Romans 7:18-19 NASB)

I dream of a church that will not tolerate gross sin in its leadership but is merciful towards the common human foibles that affect us all.

The Law

Some Christians believe the law is bad.

"... the law is holy, and the commandment is holy, righteous and good." (Romans 7:12 NIV)

What then is the problem? We are the problem.

"For what the law could not do in that it was weak through the flesh, God did by sending His own Son in the likeness of sinful flesh, on account of sin: He condemned sin in the flesh, that the righteous requirement of the law

might be fulfilled in us who do not walk according to the flesh but according to the Spirit." (Romans 8:3-4 NKJV)

I dream of a church that walks according to the Spirit.

"And I am convinced that nothing can ever separate us from God's love. Neither death nor life, neither angels nor demons, neither our fears for today nor our worries about tomorrow—not even the powers of hell can separate us from God's love." (Romans 8:38 NLT)

Simplicity

We have so complicated Christianity, when it is so simple that a child could understand.

"Because if you confess with your mouth 'Jesus is Lord' and in your heart you have faith that God raised him from the dead, you will be saved." (Romans 10:9 CEB)

I dream of a church that makes the simple message of the Bible plain for the simplest, and challenging enough for the most intelligent.

The Word

Bad preaching may be a motivational speech, a series of stories, jokes or something else just pulled out of thin air and blamed on the Holy Spirit. Yet, there is good preaching.

"How can people have faith in the Lord and ask him to save them, if they have never heard about him? And how can they hear, unless someone tells them? And how can anyone tell them without being sent by the Lord? The Scriptures say it is a beautiful sight to see even the feet of someone coming to preach the good news." (Romans 10:14-15 CEV)

I dream of a church where the Bible is preached and expounded, as in Nehemiah's simple outline of preaching.

"They read in the book, in the law of God, distinctly; and they gave the sense, so that they understood the reading." (Nehemiah 8:8 WEB)

I also dream of a receptive church, very much unlike ancient Israel.

"I have spread out My hands all day long to a disobedient and obstinate people." (Romans 10:21 NASB)

Sacrifice

The spirit of the law, the whole law, includes the sacrificial system. Our ultimate sacrifice is Jesus, but we too are encouraged to be self-sacrificial.

"I beseech you therefore, brethren, by the mercies of God, that ye present your bodies a living sacrifice, holy, acceptable unto God, which is your reasonable service." (Romans 12:1 KJV)

I dream of a church where everybody willingly serves, so that the burden is shared.

Civil Law

"Let every person be subject to the governing authorities. For there is no authority except from God, and those that exist have been instituted by God." (Romans 13:1 ESV)

I dream of a church where everyone obeys the speed limit, vaccination mandates, pays taxes and willingly upholds any other civil law that does not violate the teachings of Jesus and the Apostles.

Non-Essentials

I dream of a church where politics and personal preferences are not foisted upon anyone.

"Accept the one whose faith is weak, without quarreling over disputable matters." (Romans 14:1 NIV)

In the early church clean and unclean meats, Saturday or Sunday worship, Passover/Easter on Nisan 14 or a floating date, were matters of personal conscience, not bossy church law.

"You, then, why do you judge your brother or sister? Or why do you treat them with contempt? For we will all stand before God's judgment seat." (Romans 14:10 NIV)

I dream of a church that returns to grace on non-essentials, matters that neither Jesus nor the Apostles commanded for the church.

Sectarianism

Why do we say we are Calvinists, Lutherans, Mennonites, or Wesleyans? It has always been a puzzle that we who are called Christians also want to name ourselves after a man, which at least in principle, the Bible specifically forbids.

"Some of you are saying, 'I am a follower of Paul.' Others are saying, 'I follow Apollos,' or 'I follow Peter,' or 'I follow only Christ.' Has Christ been divided into factions?" (1 Corinthians 1:12-13a NLT)

I dream of a church that is not divided by the theology of any man.

A Humble Church

Who are we?

"For you see your calling, brothers, that not many are wise according to the flesh, not many mighty, and not many noble; but God chose the foolish things of the world that he might put to shame those who are wise. God chose the weak things of the world that he might put to shame the things that are strong." (1Corinthians 1:26-27 WEB)

I dream of a church that is not filled with ignorant know-it-alls, but is humble, realizing that we are the foolish and weak of the world.

Christ's Mind

On the other hand, let's not discredit the gift that God has given us.

"But we have the mind of Christ." (1 Corinthians 2:16 CEB)

I dream of a church that is not ashamed of that which has been given them from heaven, but in all humility judges things with the wisdom of heaven, the mind of Christ.

The Foundation

Whether we build with early church fathers, later ecumenical councils, a Reformation or something totally new, there is no other foundation upon which to build.

"... because Christ is the only foundation." (1 Corinthians 3:11 CEV)

I dream of a church that is continually in repentant revision regarding its theology, not by going to the world as modernists do, but by continually returning to what Jesus and the Apostles taught, the essentials of our common faith.

Excommunication

Though a rare step, expelling someone from the church is sometimes a wise course of action. Paul had to do it to a man who was sleeping with his mother-in-law.

"Let him who has done this be removed from among you." (1 Corinthians 5:2 ESV)

Many modern churches are afraid to remove those who commit gross public sexual sins, and sometimes even promote them to high office. I dream of a church that shows love to sexual sinners, by addressing their self-destructive behavior rather than ignoring it or pretending that it is okay.

Old Leaven

During the spring Passover festival, people purged their homes of leavening or yeast for making bread. In a similar manner, Paul encourages us.

"Therefore let us keep the feast, not with old leaven, neither with the leaven of malice and wickedness; but with the unleavened bread of sincerity and truth." (1 Corinthians 5:8 KJV)

I dream of a church that highly values sincerity and truth.

A Holy Church

Contrary to some churches, Paul instructs us.

"Do not be deceived; neither the sexually immoral, nor idolaters, nor adulterers, nor homosexuals, nor thieves, nor the greedy, nor those habitually drunk, nor verbal abusers, nor

swindlers, will inherit the kingdom of God." (1 Corinthians 6:9b-10 NASB)

I dream of a church that values holy living.

Marriage and Celibacy

Some have a gift of celibacy allowing them to devote their entire existence to God. Others may later discover a need to be married, and because of this nobody should ever be encouraged to make an irreversible vow of celibacy, but given freedom to change their minds if they later so choose.

"But if they cannot control themselves, they should marry, for it is better to marry than to burn with passion." (1 Corinthians 7:9 NIV)

This is not possible for those who have made an unwise oath. I dream of a church where celibates and married are honored, and that people are not coerced into making foolish vows, but are always free to change their minds if they later want to become married.

Pay

Some churches can afford to pay well, but value pastoral work so little that they pay only a pittance.

"For it is written in the law of Moses, 'You shall not muzzle an ox while it treads out the grain.' Is it oxen God is concerned about? Or does He say it altogether for our sakes? For our sakes, no doubt, this is written, that he who plows should plow in hope, and he who threshes in hope should be partaker of his hope. If we have sown spiritual things for you, is it a great thing if we reap your material things? If others are partakers of this right over you, are we not even more?" (1 Corinthians 9:9-12 NKJV)

I dream of a church that values its pastors so highly, that they don't have to waste precious time making tents as Paul did.

Baptism

Although baptize literally means immerse, it is not always used literally.

"In the cloud and in the sea, all of them were baptized as followers of Moses." (1 Corinthians 10:2 NLT)

Adults and children were baptized, having gone through the red sea dry shod. How was Jesus baptized?

"And when Jesus was baptized, immediately he went up from the water" (Matthew 3:16a ESV)

The Greek literally says, He went up "away from" the water. It could have been ankle deep. Without details, we simply don't know anything except that water was used. I dream of a church that does not impose a particular age or mode of baptism that the Bible does not, but leaves it up to the faith of individual members.

Hair Length

The topic of hair length may seem to be legalism, but remember this is the New Testament. Legalism has to do with the letter of Old Testament law. Paul recommends that under normal circumstances men have shorter hair and women longer hair. Some may claim this was just constrained by culture, contradicting Paul.

"This is how things are done in all of God's churches, and that's why none of you should argue about what I have said." (1 Corinthians 11:16 CEV)

I dream of a church that believes every word of God and simply obeys without arguing.

Communion

Communion is not a private meal, but a community meal. It is a mystery, called a sacrament in the west, because Jesus said, *"This is my body... This is my blood"*

It is an ordinance, because Jesus said, *"Eat this... Drink this..."*

It is a memorial, because Jesus said, *"remember me." (1 Corinthians 11:23-26 CEV)*

It is a time for self-examination, *"Let a person examine himself, then, and so eat of the bread and drink of the cup." (1 Corinthians 11:28 ESV)*

It is a time to *"wait for one another." (1 Corinthians 11:33 NASB)*

I dream of a church that discerns the body of Christ in each other and humbly waits for each other.

Gifts

God's gifts are too many to count, but some are mentioned by Paul. Some seem to think that all should be able to speak with tongues, but we are not all a foot, a hand, an ear or an eye.

"Are all apostles? are all prophets? are all teachers? are all workers of miracles? Have all the gifts of healing? do all speak with tongues? do all interpret?" (1 Corinthians 12:29-30 KJV)

I dream of a gifted church without jealousy or competition, but respect for each other's abilities as unique and given by God.

Love

I dream of a church where love prevails.

"Love is patient, love is kind, it is not jealous; love does not brag, it is not arrogant. It does not act disgracefully, it does not seek its own benefit; it is not provoked, does not keep an account of a wrong suffered, it does not rejoice in unrighteousness, but rejoices with the truth; it keeps every confidence, it believes all things, hopes all things, endures all things." (1 Corinthians 13:4-7 NASB)

Prophecy

Powerful preaching is a gift to the church.

"But the one who prophesies speaks to people for their strengthening, encouraging and comfort." (1 Corinthians 14:3 NIV)

I dream of a church that preaches the Word of God in both private and public prophesying.

Women

There is a lot of anger in feminism. We show our sisters in the faith brotherly love, but it's not hate speech to lovingly disagree. Do we trust God enough to disregard the propaganda of the world around us? Do we believe that God inspired Paul?

"Let your women keep silent in the churches, for they are not permitted to speak; but they are to be submissive, as the law also says. And if they want to learn something, let them ask their own husbands at home; for it is shameful for women to speak in church." (1 Corinthians 14:34-35 NKJV)

Do we trust that God inspired this in love for women and not to "oppress" them as modern propaganda might say? Are any men who do not preach somehow "oppressed"? Do we trust that obedience to God produces happiness for all?

So, what about women prophets, of which there are several in the New Testament? Harmonizing these seemingly contradictory facts is really quite simple. A prophetess does not have to speak publicly to share her prophecy or give inspired advice.

I dream of a church with simple trust that God will bless us wonderfully when we stand behind our men as congregational leaders.

Gospel

The Gospel can be summarized simply as follows.

"Christ died for our sins, just as the Scriptures said. He was buried, and he was raised from the dead on the third day, just as the Scriptures said." (1 Corinthians 15:3b-4 NLT)

I dream of a church that can explain the Gospel to others in such simple terms.

Resurrection

Progressives who deny the resurrection have not introduced anything new but have regressed to old sins.

"Now if Christ is preached, that he has been raised from the dead, how do some among you say that there is no resurrection of the dead? But if there is no resurrection of the dead, neither has Christ been raised. If Christ has not been raised, then our preaching is in vain, and your faith also is in vain." (1 Corinthians 15:12-14 WEB)

I dream of a church that believes in Jesus' resurrection and awaits the resurrection at His return.

"Our dead and decaying bodies will be changed into bodies that won't die or decay." (vs 53 CEV)

Financial Matters

Elders of the church must keep their hands off when it comes to church finances. Choosing who will be in charge of finances is an area for a congregational decision, so that not even a suspicion of impropriety can be accused of the elders.

"I'll send whomever you approve to Jerusalem with letters of recommendation to bring your gift." (1 Corinthians 16:3b CEB)

I dream of a church where finances are handled by those the congregation approves.

Salvation

Many Christians have read *"now is the day of salvation"* (2 Corinthians 6:2 ESV) and haven't read the rest of the Bible on the topic. In Greek it's actually *"a day of salvation."* Naïve people ask, "Have you been saved?" The wise Bible student answers, "I **am** saved, **am being** saved and **will be** saved." The guy who knows his Bible is correct. We **are saved** (Luke 19:9; Romans 8:24; 10:10; 2 Corinthians 6:2; Ephesians 2:5, 8; 2 Timothy 1:9; Titus 3:5; 1

Peter 3:21), **are being** saved (1 Corinthians 1:18; 15:2; 2 Corinthians 2:15; Philippians 2:12), and **will be** saved (Matthew 1:21; 10:22; 24:13; Mark 13:13; 16:16; John 10:9; Acts 2:21; 11:14; 15:11; 16:31; Romans 5:10; 1 Thessalonians 5:8).

I dream of a church that knows its Bible well.

Another Jesus

Some use Jesus' name, but present a false Christ.

"For such are false apostles, deceitful workers, transforming themselves into the apostles of Christ. And no marvel; for Satan himself is transformed into an angel of light." (2 Corinthians 11:13-14 KJV)

I dream of a church that knows its Bible so well that false prophets make no headway.

Galatianism

Paul went to Jerusalem to consult with the other Apostles about Galatian legalism.

"We went there because of those who pretended to be followers and had sneaked in among us as spies. They had come to take away the freedom that Christ Jesus had given

us, and they were trying to make us their slaves." (Galatians 2:4 CEV)

I dream of a church that follows the teachings of Jesus and the Apostles and not the letter of the law or religious rules made up by men.

Foundation

Upon what is the church built?

"... built on the foundation of the apostles and prophets, Christ Jesus himself being the cornerstone" (Ephesians 2:20 ESV).

It is for that reason that Protestants use the term sola scriptura, the scriptures alone. I dream of a church that has as its sole foundation the New and Old Testaments, and the four Gospels as the cornerstone.

Unity

Church unity is not found in uniform doctrines or practices, although there is remarkable unity in what is really essential. The Holy Spirit has made sure of that.

"Endeavouring to keep the unity of the Spirit in the bond of peace. There is one body, and one Spirit, even as ye are called in one hope of your calling; One Lord, one faith, one baptism, One God and Father of all, who is above all,

and *through all, and in you all." (Ephesians 4:3-6 KJV)*

How is unity even possible considering disagreements over doctrine. It is found in the bond of peace not twigs of doctrine. I dream of a church at peace with all Christians who believe the essentials taught by Jesus and the Apostles. I dream of a church that is gracious about non-essentials that neither Jesus nor the Apostles commanded.

Husbands and Wives

There is a very misunderstood point in today's culture, but it is taught in the Bible several times (Ephesians 5:22, 24; Colossians 3:18; 1 Peter 3:1-6). Wives submit does not mean becoming doormats or allowing a man to abuse you. Absolutely not! What it means is to be a team player, supportive, encouraging, not someone who constantly undermines her man. Men, this is addressed to women, not you. It is and must be her choice, not coerced by a domineering husband.

"A husband is the head of his wife like Christ is head of the church, that is, the savior of the body." (Ephesians 5:23 CEB)

Who is the head? How is this headship expressed? Proper headship is exemplified by *"submitting to one another in the fear of God."* *(Ephesians 5:21 NKJV)* Does Jesus submit to the needs of His Bride, the church?

"Husbands, love your wives, just as Christ also loved the church and gave Himself up for her" *(vs 25 NASB). "Husbands, likewise, dwell with them with understanding, giving honor to the wife, as to the weaker vessel, and as being heirs together of the grace of life, that your prayers may not be hindered." (1 Peter 3:7 NKJV)*

I dream of a church where husbands and wives have abandoned the deceptive marital advice of a world where half of marriages fail, and devoted themselves to trusting that God knows best.

Citizenship

In highly nationalistic countries, citizenship and Christianity are often confused.

"But our citizenship is in heaven." (Philippians 3:20a NIV)

I dream of a church where the love of neighbors goes beyond national borders.

Positive Thinking

Happy pills can overcome depression for a short time, but according to medical science, in the long term we need to change to positive thinking. It may not be such new science, but very ancient.

"Finally, brethren, whatever things are true, whatever things are noble, whatever things are just, whatever things are pure, whatever things are lovely, whatever things are of good report, if there is any virtue and if there is anything praiseworthy—meditate on these things." (Philippians 4:8 NKJV)

I dream of a church that is not afraid of painful truths, but also faces them with a positive attitude.

Forbearing

One of the great keys to church success is forbearance.

"Make allowance for each other's faults, and forgive anyone who offends you. Remember, the Lord forgave you, so you must forgive others." (Colossians 3:13 NLT)

I dream of a church where each member bears with the other and forgiveness reigns.

Prophetic Speculation

Some churches get caught up in fantastic theories about prophecy and the return of Jesus Christ.

"But concerning the times and the seasons, brothers, you have no need that anything be written to you. For you yourselves know well that the day of the Lord comes like a thief in the night." (1 Thessalonians 5:1-2 WEB)

I dream of a church that is balanced and understands that the biggest key is not setting dates, figuring out who the beast or the false prophet is, or what 666 means, but being ready always.

"So then, let's not sleep like the others, but let's stay awake and stay sober." (vs 6 CEB)

Overseers

Many churches today completely ignore the biblical qualifications for ordination, because they are offended by them. Why?

"... the husband of one wife... He must manage his own household well" (1 Timothy 3:2-7 ESV)

It refers to males. Male leadership has been God's pattern from ancient Israel to Jesus' choice of apostles to most of Christian history with very few exceptions. Many Protestant churches have long forgotten the Reformation, becoming part of more of a Deformation. They are put to shame by the ancient churches, which have not yet compromised on this point.

I dream of a church where men and women trust God to have given us church leadership which is best for all.

Liturgy

What should be some main points in a church's outline of service?

"Until I come, devote yourself to the public reading of Scripture, to exhortation, to teaching." (1 Timothy 4:13 ESV)

I dream of a church that includes these simple points in its liturgy or service outline.

Scripture

While many churches use the Bible like a menu, picking and choosing what they can agree with, Paul had a different view.

"All Scripture is God-breathed and is useful for teaching, rebuking, correcting and training in righteousness, 17 so that the servant of God may be thoroughly equipped for every good work." (2 Timothy 3:16-17 NIV)

I dream of a church that actually believes the Bible is God's Word, all of it, that understands different genres, but does not use that as an excuse to dilute it.

Elders

In the early church overseer and elder were synonymous. Again Paul reiterates God's instruction that the elder must be *"the husband of one wife" (Titus 1:6 NASB)*

I dream of a church that takes God's Word at face value.

Dissenters

Every church has probably experienced divisive and disruptive people.

"Reject a divisive man after the first and second admonition, knowing that such a person is warped and sinning, being self-condemned." (Titus 3:10-11 NKJV)

I dream of a church that is not afraid to curtail such people.

Rest

Though a day off is good for body and soul, our Sabbath rest is no longer in a day but in Jesus Christ (Matthew 11:28-30). Under Moses, a generation of Sabbath-keeping Israelites did not enter the land of rest, because they rebelled. Under Joshua, the following generation of Sabbath keepers entered the land of rest, but he spoke of another day of rest (Hebrews 3-4).

"So there is a special rest still waiting for the people of God." (Hebrews 4:9 NLT)

I dream of a church that focuses more on our eternal Sabbath rest, than a letter-of-the-law day.

A Knowledgeable Church

Too many Christians today are ignorant of their Bibles. The anonymous writer of Hebrews was also disappointed with early Christians.

"In fact, though by this time you ought to be teachers, you need someone to teach you the elementary truths of God's word all over again. You need milk, not solid food!" (Hebrews 5:12 NIV)

In a world where many churches only preach short sermons filled with empty platitudes a proper foundation was never laid.

"... the foundation of repentance from dead works and of faith toward God, of the doctrine

of baptisms, of laying on of hands, of resurrection of the dead, and of eternal judgment." (Hebrews 6:1b-2 NKJV)

I dream of a church that reads and discusses the Bible and where Bible classes are packed with eager students.

Tithing

There is no direct command to tithe given to the church. Jesus did tell the scribes and Pharisees who were still under the law, that they should tithe (Matthew 23:23). However, the priesthood changed from Melchizedek to the Levites and is now given to Jesus.

"The priests who collect tithes are men who die, so Melchizedek is greater than they are, because we are told that he lives on." (Hebrews 7:8 NLT)

I dream of a church that does not need a command, but is of a willing heart that generously tithes to bless Jesus' ministry on earth, because we recognize His priesthood.

"You are a priest forever in the order of Melchizedek." (vs 17b)

Faith

When we speak of a community of faith, we look at those who have gone on before us (Hebrews 11). We acknowledge them.

"... we are surrounded by so great a cloud of witnesses" (Hebrews 12:1 WEB).

I dream of a church that believes and trusts God as they did.

Support Your Leaders

Oh how joyful it is to be in a church where the leaders are loved and encouraged, and how stressful and sorrowful it is when self-willed rebels ruin a church.

"Obey your spiritual leaders, and do what they say. Their work is to watch over your souls, and they are accountable to God. Give them reason to do this with joy and not with sorrow. That would certainly not be for your benefit." *(Hebrews 13:17 NLT)*

I dream of a church where the whole congregation supports a unified vision given by God to its leaders.

Temptation

We are all tempted, but we don't all give in to it.

"But each person is tempted when he is lured and enticed by his own desire. Then desire when it has conceived gives birth to sin, and sin when it is fully grown brings forth death." (James 1:14-15 ESV)

So, the process is simple: lust allowed to fester brings sin and sin allowed to fester brings death. I dream of a church that is learning to stop temptation in its tracks before sin is conceived.

Doers

The Bible is practical, not just theory.

"You must be doers of the word and not only hearers who mislead themselves." (James 1:22 CEB)

I dream of a church that puts the Bible into practice.

Religion

The word religion is misused in popular Christianity. People forget that James encourages religion.

"Religion that pleases God the Father must be pure and spotless. You must help needy orphans and widows and not let this world make you evil." (James 1:27 CEV)

I dream of a church that does not avoid religion, but practices pure religion.

The Poor

Dishonoring the poor is still common practice in our world. Yet, we Christians are to be different.

"God has given a lot of faith to the poor people in this world. He has also promised them a share in his kingdom that he will give to everyone who loves him." (James 2:5b CEV)

I dream of a church that honors the poor as equals.

Living Faith

Many Christians seem to have a dead faith and some evangelists encourage an "easy believism" without repentance. Yet, faith that saves has fruits.

"What good is it, my brothers, if someone says he has faith but does not have works? Can that faith save him? If a brother or sister is poorly clothed and lacking in daily food, and one of

you says to them, 'Go in peace, be warmed and filled,' without giving them the things needed for the body, what good is that? So also faith by itself, if it does not have works, is dead. But someone will say, 'You have faith and I have works.' Show me your faith apart from your works, and I will show you my faith by my works." (James 2:14-18 ESV)

I dream of a church with a living faith, seen in its good works.

The Flapping Tongue

Many churches have been ruined by gossip.

"Even so the tongue is a little member, and boasteth great things. Behold, how great a matter a little fire kindleth! And the tongue is a fire, a world of iniquity" (James 3:5-6a KJV)

I dream of a church where people can hold their tongues and keep gossip under control.

Overcoming Evil

People often wonder about how to overcome the devil. It's not complicated.

"Submit therefore to God. But resist the devil, and he will flee from you." (James 4:7 NASB)

I dream of a church that submits to God and resists the devil.

Anointing

How often do modern Christians practice anointing the sick? In some churches it's just not known.

"Is anyone among you sick? Let them call the elders of the church to pray over them and anoint them with oil in the name of the Lord." *(James 5:14 NIV)*

I dream of a church where there is faith to anoint the sick.

Living Stones

In masonry, a living stone is one that is easily workable, to chip into shape and fit a particular wall space.

"Coming to Him as to a living stone, rejected indeed by men, but chosen by God and precious, you also, as living stones, are being built up a spiritual house, a holy priesthood, to offer up spiritual sacrifices acceptable to God through Jesus Christ." *(1 Peter 2: 4-5 NKJV)*

I dream of a church where each member is workable, fitting in well with the team.

Personal Growth

A growing Christian is a blessing to all.

"Supplement your faith with a generous provision of moral excellence, and moral excellence with knowledge, and knowledge with self-control, and self-control with patient endurance, and patient endurance with godliness, and godliness with brotherly affection, and brotherly affection with love for everyone." (2 Peter 1:5b-7 NLT)

I dream of a church where individual growth in every member is visible.

False Teachers

False teachers denigrate the Bible as merely the will of men filled with private interpretations. Peter contradicts that kind of blubber.

"knowing this first, that no prophecy of Scripture is of private interpretation. For no prophecy ever came by the will of man: but holy men of God spoke, being moved by the Holy Spirit." (2 Peter 1:20-21 WEB)

We should not be shocked. Such things were foretold.

"But false prophets also arose among the people. In the same way, false teachers will come among you. They will introduce destructive opinions and deny the master who bought them, bringing quick destruction on themselves. Many will follow them in their unrestrained immorality, and because of these false teachers the way of truth will be slandered. In their greed they will take advantage of you with lies. The judgment pronounced against them long ago hasn't fallen idle, nor is their destruction sleeping." (2 Peter 2:1-3 CEB)

I dream of a church that believes that the Bible is God-breathed, not mere human opinions and is therefore not deceived by false teachers.

Love in Action

Real love is seen in deeds, not just words.

"We know what love is because Jesus gave his life for us. That's why we must give our lives for each other. If we have all we need and see one of our own people in need, we must have pity on that person, or else we cannot say we love God. Children, you show love for others by truly helping them, and not merely by talking about it." (1 John 3:16-18 CEV) "If anyone says, 'I love God,' and hates his

brother, he is a liar; for he who does not love his brother whom he has seen cannot love God whom he has not seen. And this commandment we have from him: whoever loves God must also love his brother." (1 John 4:20-21 ESV)

I dream of a church that exhibits love in action.

Contend for the Faith

Many wonder what is the standard of Christian faith. Jude makes no mistake about it, urging us all to fight for the faith already given.

"... contend earnestly for the faith that was once for all time handed down to the saints." (Jude 1:3 NASB)

I dream of a church that understands the holy deposit laid down by Jesus and the Apostles as that which was once for all entrusted to the saints.

Seven Churches

One of the greatest lessons of the seven churches is that six of the seven had major problems, possibly a prophecy of the church throughout history. Ephesus left its first love, Smyrna was persecuted, Pergamos compromised, Thyatira was corrupt, Sardis was dead, Philadelphia was faithful and Laodicea was lukewarm. Each is told, *"To him who overcomes … "* (Revelation 2:7, 11, 17, 26; 3:5, 12, 21) and various rewards in eternal life are given. Even faithful Philadelphia has things to overcome.

Like the seven churches, church history does little to praise men and much to reveal how much grace God has shown.

I dream of a church that, no matter its local circumstances, is an overcoming church.

The Woman

The woman in Revelation 12 is more than Mary giving birth to Jesus, but also Eve and Israel and the Church.

"And I will put enmity between you [the snake] and the woman, and between your offspring and hers; he will crush your head, and you will strike his heel." (Genesis 3:15 NIV)

The stars once pictured the tribes of Israel (Genesis 37:9-10) and so the woman is crowned with the twelve tribes and now the twelve apostles. I dream of a church that is crowned with the teachings of the apostles, that defeats the devil by the blood of the Lamb and by their testimony, and does not love their lives so much they are afraid to die. (Revelation 12:1-12)

Praise

John saw a great choir of overcomers in heaven singing.

"Great and marvelous are your works, Lord God, the Almighty! Righteous and true are your ways, you King of the nations. Who wouldn't fear you, Lord, and glorify your name? For you only are holy. For all the nations will come and worship before you. For your righteous acts have been revealed." (Revelation 15:3b-4 WEB)

I dream of a church that sings to God with greater heart than found at any sports event.

Babylon

Greed fuels corrupt politics and false religion. Yet, this world's Babylonian system is about to die.

"The merchants of the earth will weep and mourn over her, for no one buys their cargoes anymore—cargoes of gold, silver, jewels, and pearls; fine linen, purple, silk, and scarlet; all those things made of scented wood, ivory, fine

wood, bronze, iron, and marble; cinnamon, incense, fragrant ointment, and frankincense; wine, oil, fine flour, and wheat; cattle, sheep, horses, and carriages; and slaves, even human lives." (Revelation 18:11-13 CEB)

At the destruction of the Babylonian political-religious system of greed and oppression, Christians sing a song of rejoicing.

"Praise the Lord! To our God belongs the glorious power to save, because his judgments are honest and fair. That filthy prostitute ruined the earth with shameful deeds. But God has judged her and made her pay the price for murdering his servants." (Revelation 19:1b-2 CEV)

I dream of a church that while living in this present Babylon is not corrupted by it.

The Bride

The church is called the Bride of Christ. The marriage supper is a time of rejoicing.

"Hallelujah! For the Lord our God the Almighty reigns. Let us rejoice and exult and give him the glory, for the marriage of the Lamb has come, and his Bride has made herself ready; it was granted her to clothe herself with fine linen, bright and pure"—for the fine linen is the

righteous deeds of the saints." (Revelation 19:6b-8 ESV)*

I dream of a church that is preparing itself for the marriage of the Lamb.

The Great White Throne

The Day of Judgment will come for everyone.

"And I saw a great white throne, and him that sat on it, from whose face the earth and the heaven fled away; and there was found no place for them. And I saw the dead, small and great, stand before God; and the books were opened: and another book was opened, which is the book of life: and the dead were judged out of those things which were written in the books, according to their works." (Revelation 20:11-12 KJV)

I dream of a church that takes this seriously and looks forward to being told, *"Well done, good and faithful servant." (Matthew 25:21 NKJV)*

Come

The invitation is open. What will you choose?

"The Spirit and the bride say, "Come." And let the one who hears say, "Come." And let the one who is thirsty come; let the one who

desires, take the water of life without cost." *(Revelation 22:17 NASB)*

I dream of a church filled with repentant people flocking in to accept God's gift of eternal life.

Postlude

A Catholic priest friend once admitted that the church is sometimes the Bride of Christ and sometimes the Whore of Babylon. I suggested in reply that the Protestant church is probably very similar. Many have been severely hurt by their church experience. Perhaps they moved on to another church. Perhaps they began a house church. Perhaps they left entirely. Whatever you have experienced, keep on being the church. Don't run back to Babylon. Keep sharing the words of life in a loving community. Keep dreaming of a pure, wholesome Bride of Christ.

Versions of the Bible Used

KJV King James Bible. Public Domain.

CEB Common English Bible (CEB) Copyright © 2011 by Common English Bible

CEV Contemporary English Version (CEV) Copyright © 1995 by American Bible Society

ESV English Standard Version (ESV) The Holy Bible, English Standard Version. ESV® Text Edition: 2016. Copyright © 2001 by Crossway Bibles, a publishing ministry of Good News Publishers.

NKJV New King James Version (NKJV) Scripture taken from the New King James Version®. Copyright © 1982 by Thomas Nelson. Used by permission. All rights reserved.

NIV Holy Bible, New International Version®, NIV® Copyright © 1973, 1978, 1984, 2011 by Biblica, Inc.® Used by permission. All rights reserved worldwide.

NLT Scripture quotations are taken from the Holy Bible, New Living Translation, copyright ©1996, 2004, 2007.Used by permission of Tyndale House Publishers, Inc., Carol Stream, Illinois 60188. All Rights Reserved.

ESV The ESV® Bible (The Holy Bible, English Standard Version®) copyright © 2001 by Crossway Bibles, a publishing ministry of Good

www.ingramcontent.com/pod-product-compliance
Lightning Source LLC
Chambersburg PA
CBHW052112150726
48002CB00006B/2326